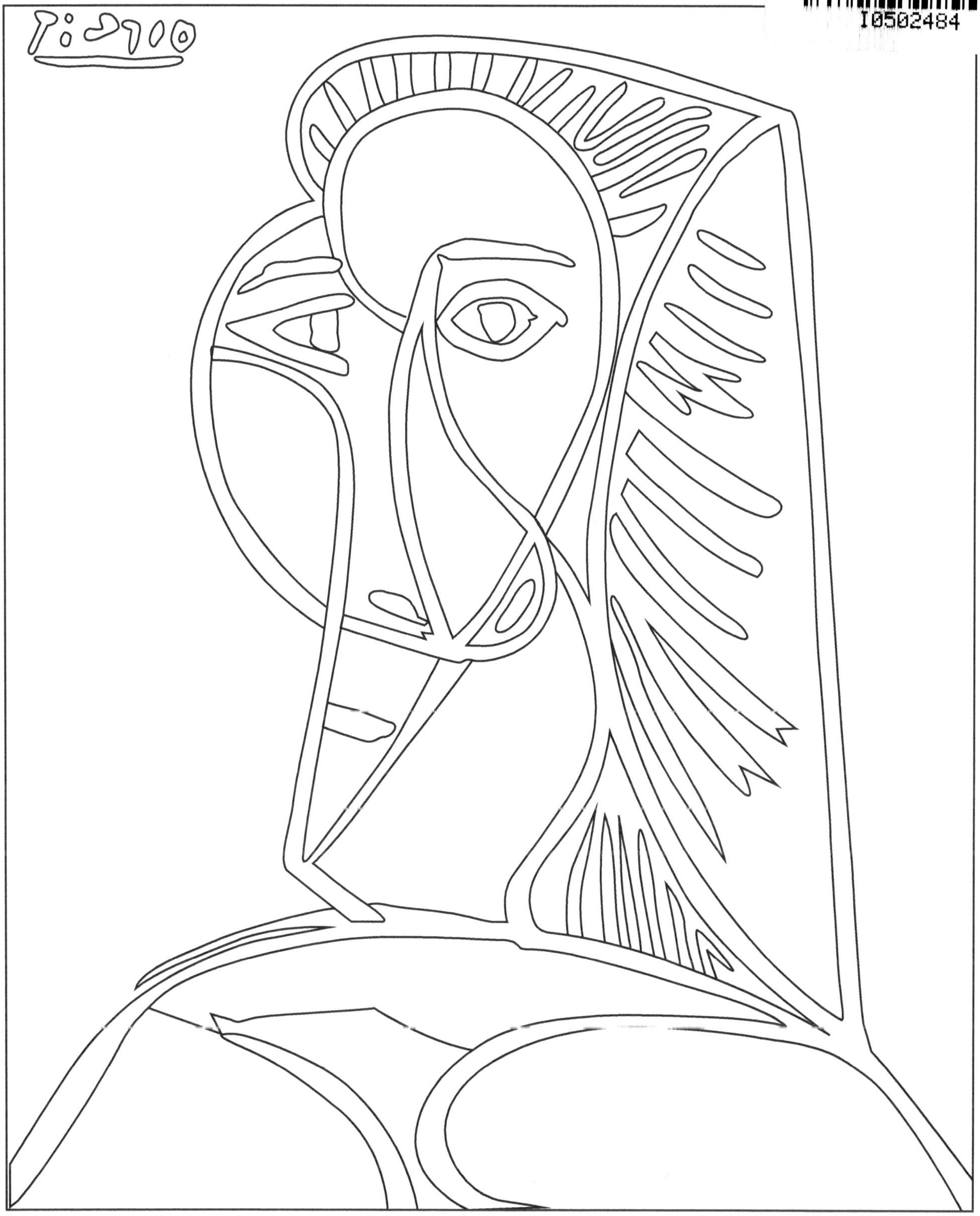

Tête de Femme (Head of a Woman)

1943

Pablo Picasso (Spanish, 1881 - 1973)

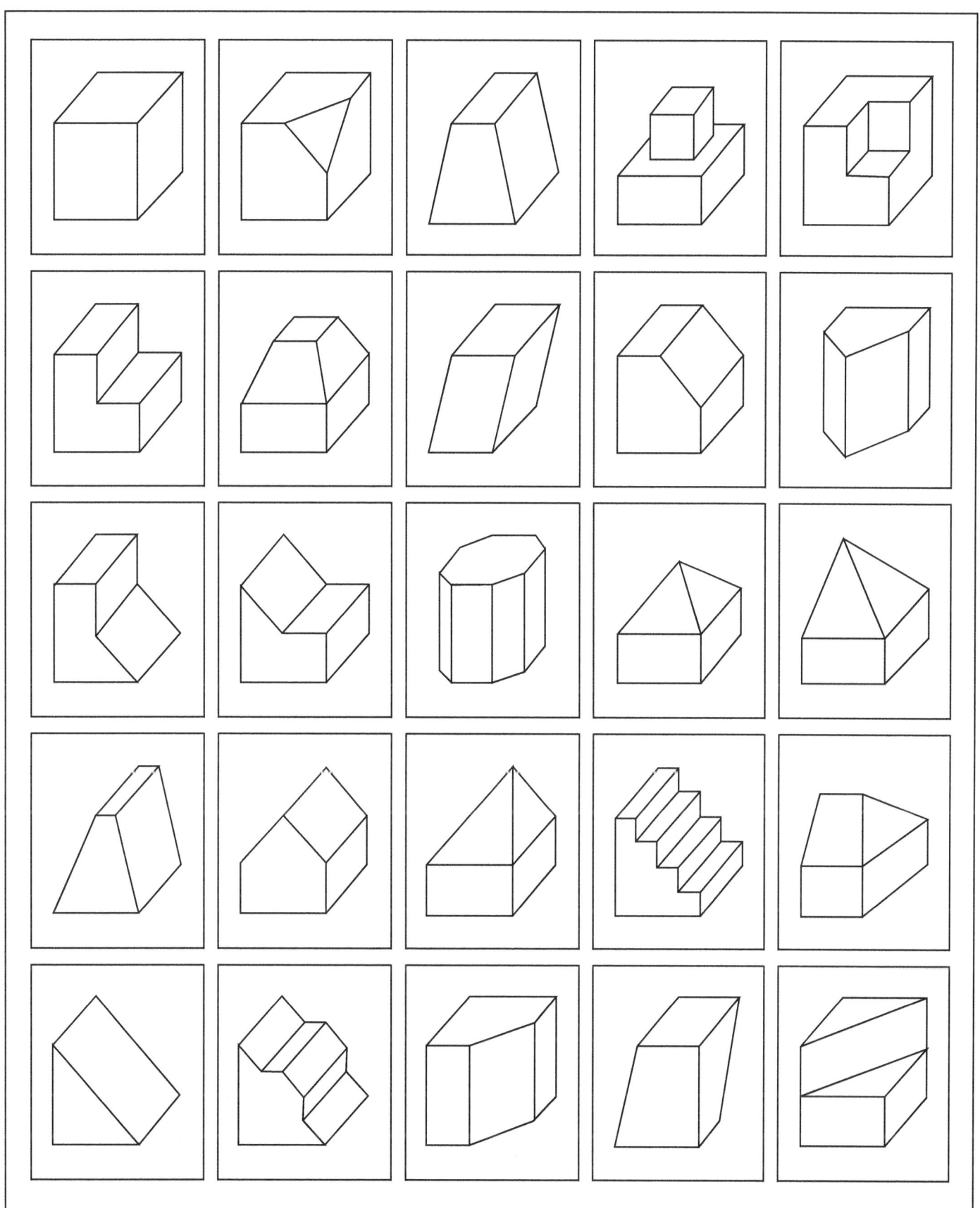

Wall Drawing #601, Forms Derived from a Cube (25 Variations)

1989

Sol LeWitt (American, 1928 - 2007)

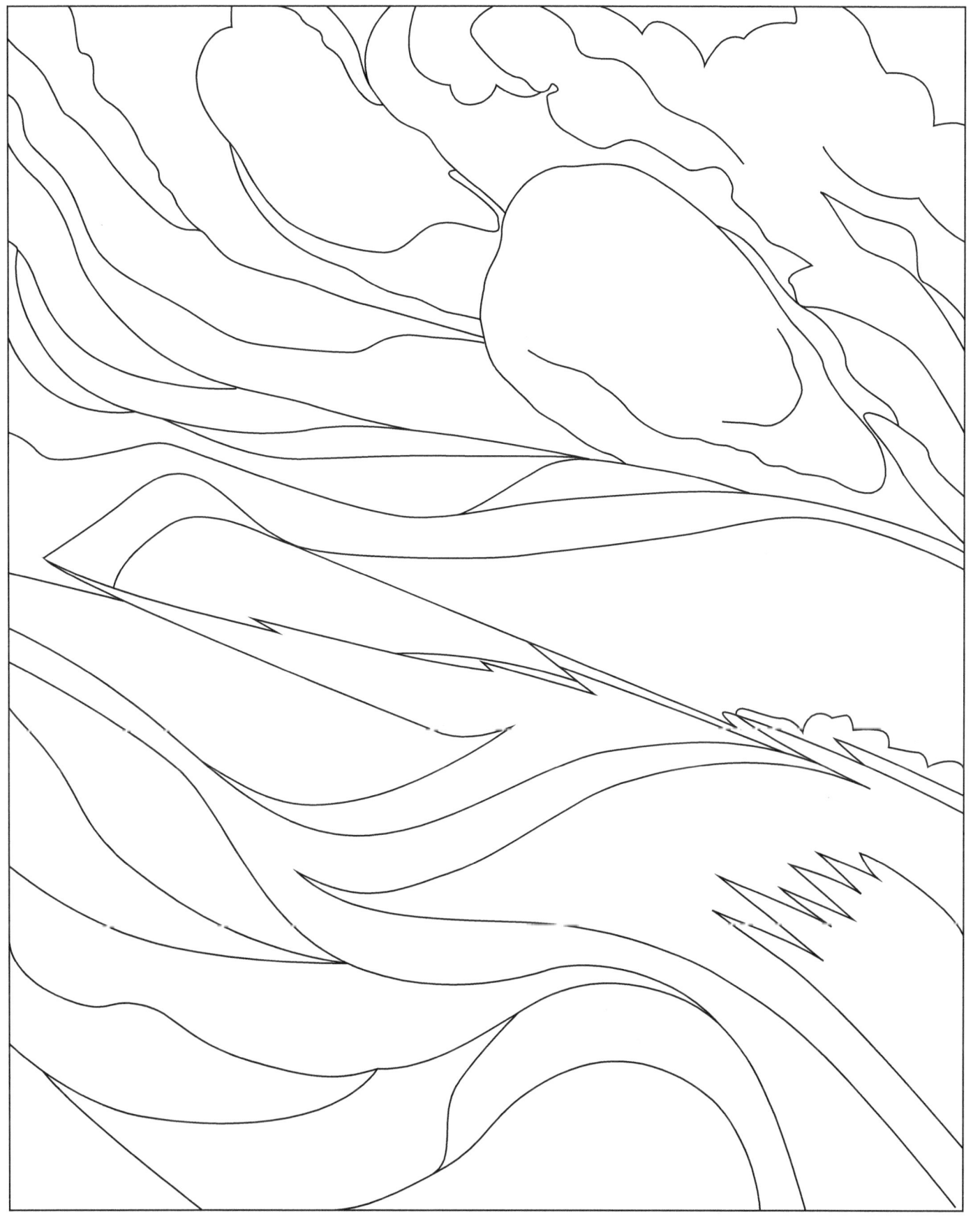

From the Lake No. 1

1924

Georgia O'Keeffe (American, 1887 - 1986)

Portraits de M.E.P... et de Mlle L.P.

(Portraits of Edouard and Marie-Louise Pailleron)

1881

Artist: John Singer Sargent (American, 1856 - 1925)

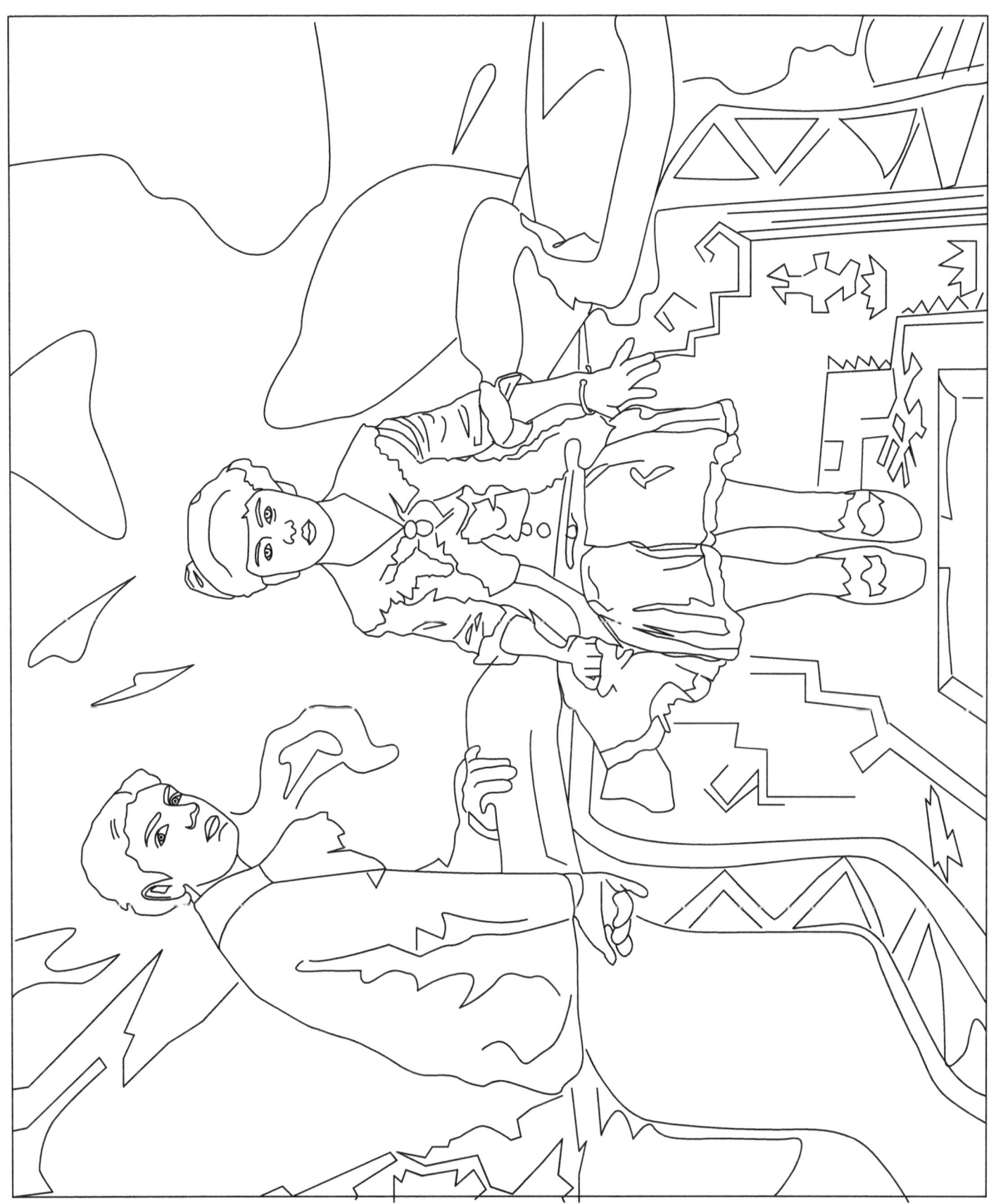

Self-Portrait
1977
Chuck Close (American, born 1940)
Printer: Crown Point Press

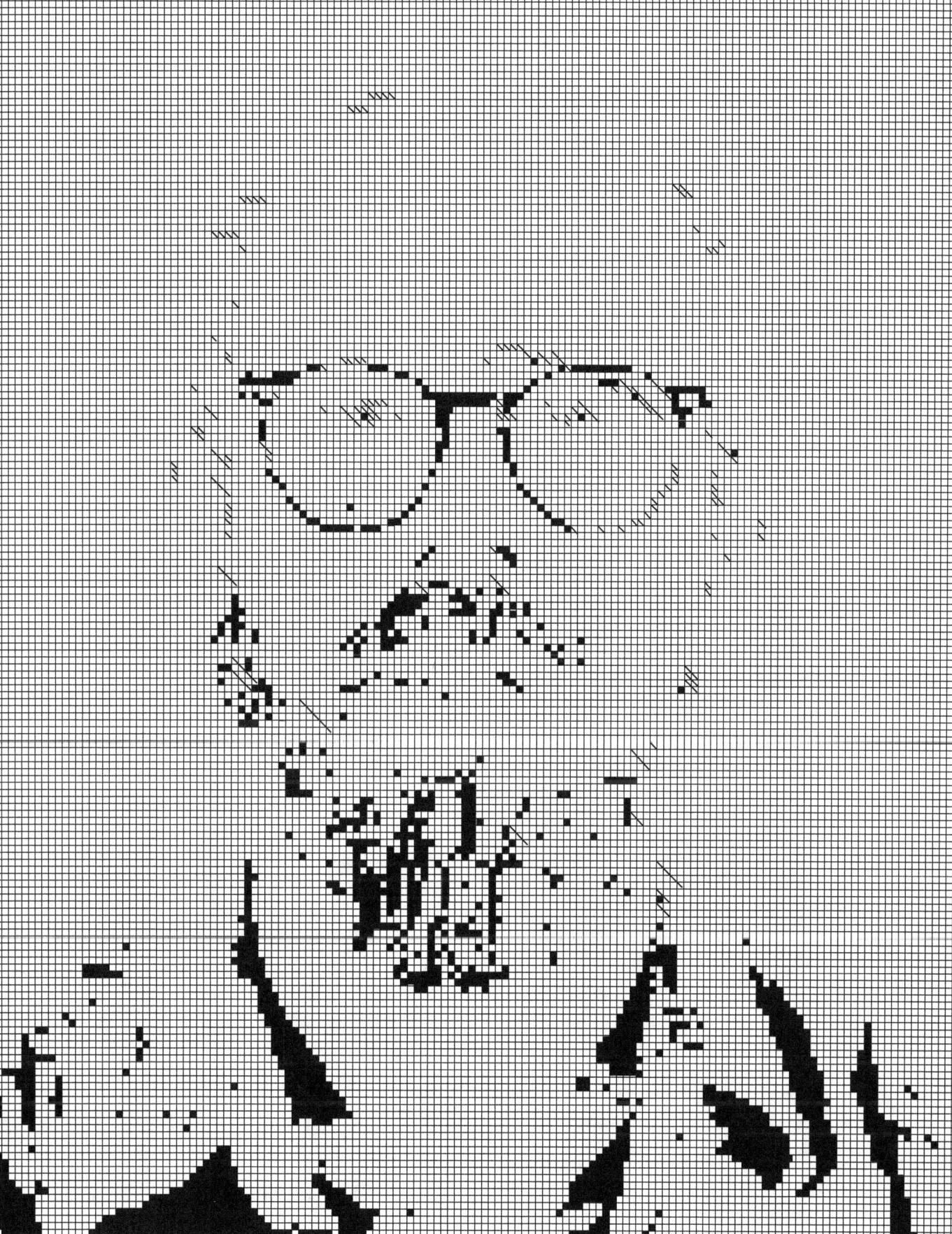

Study After Velásquez's Portrait of Pope Innocent X
1953
Francis Bacon (English, 1909 - 1992)

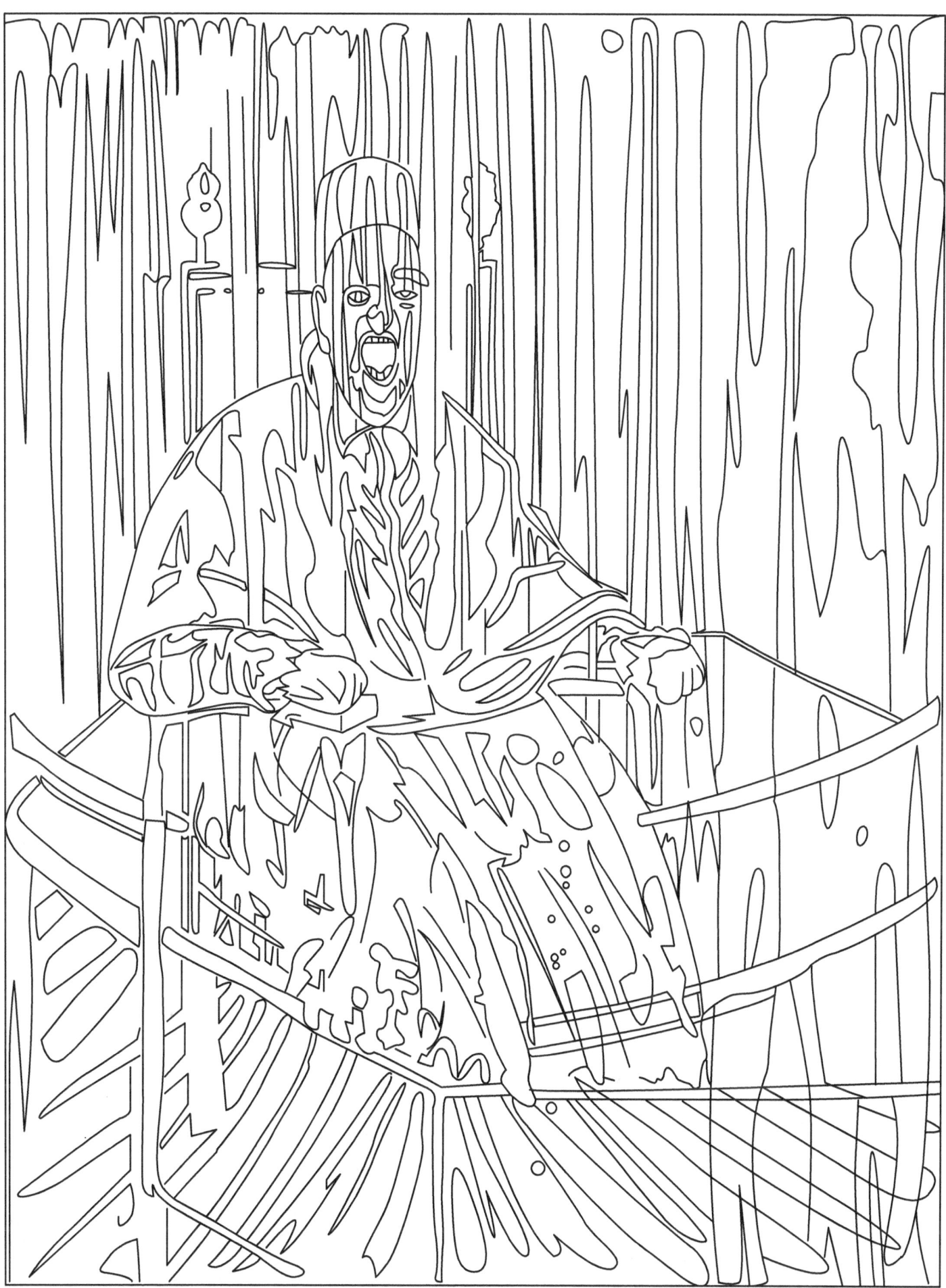

Mao
1972
Andy Warhol (American, 1928 - 1987)

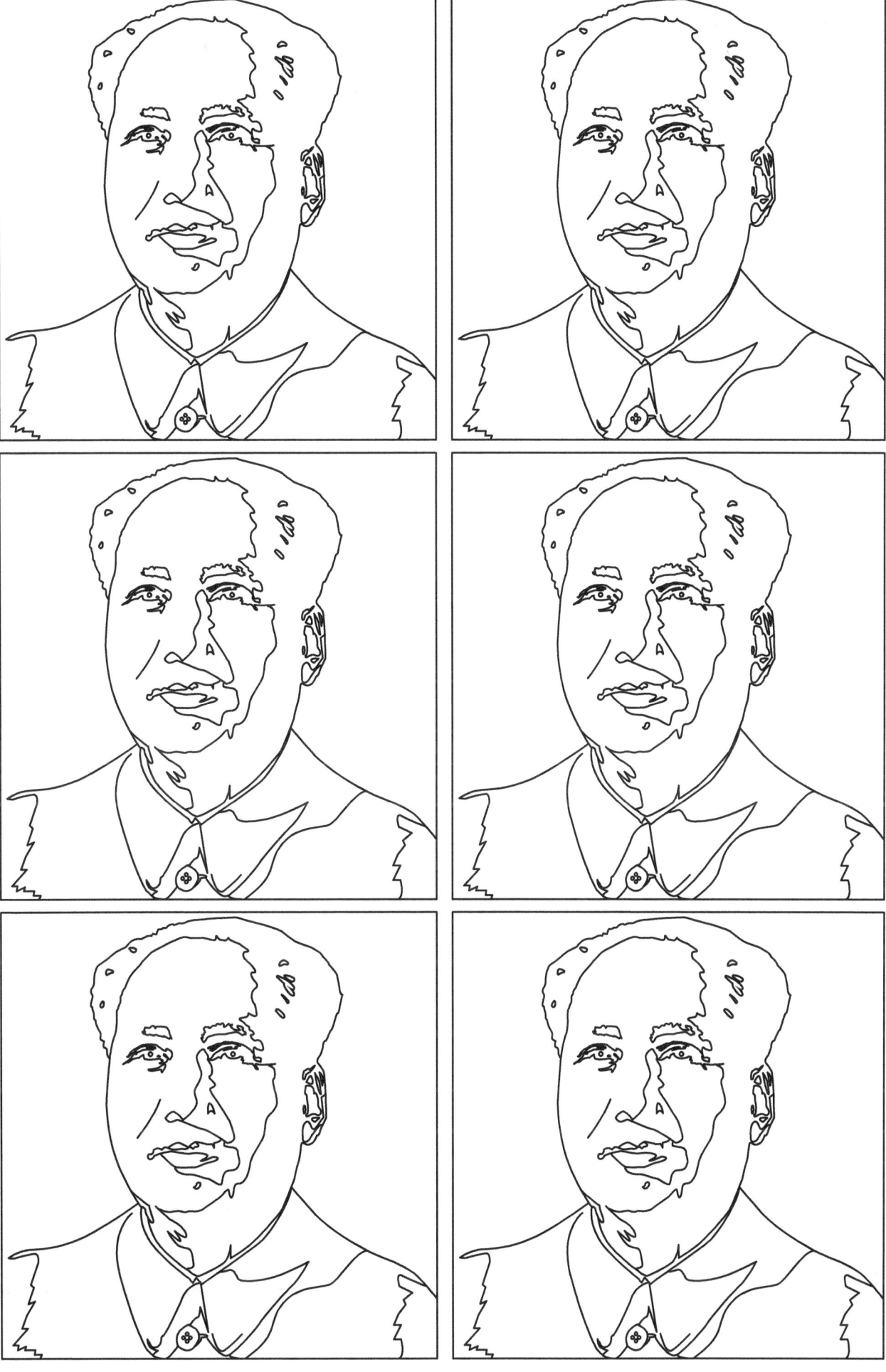

Amazing Juggler
1952
Yasuo Kuniyoshi (American, born Japan, 1889 - 1953)

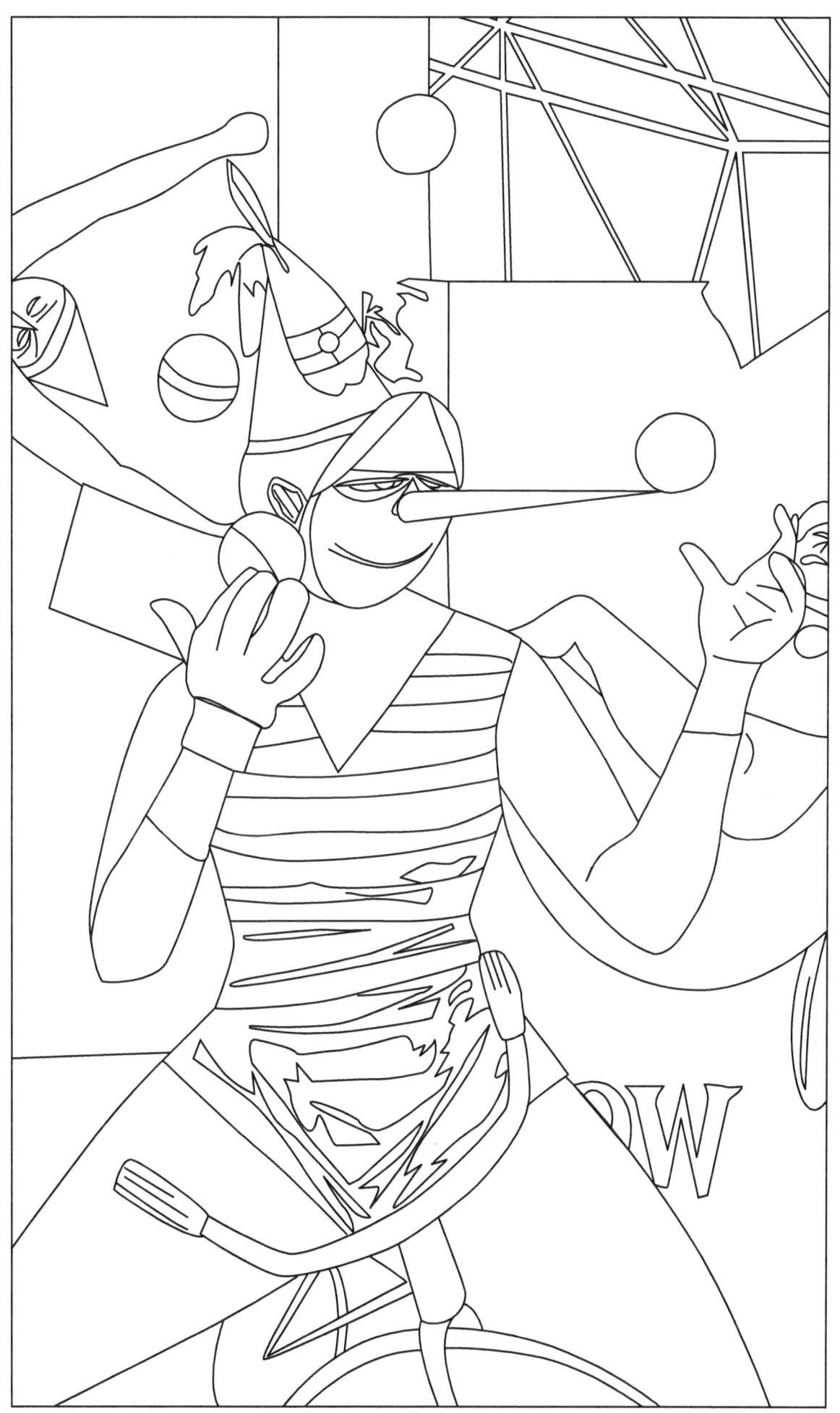

Untitled
1984
Jean-Michel Basquiat (American, 1960 - 1988)

Automat
1927

Edward Hopper (American, 1882 - 1967)

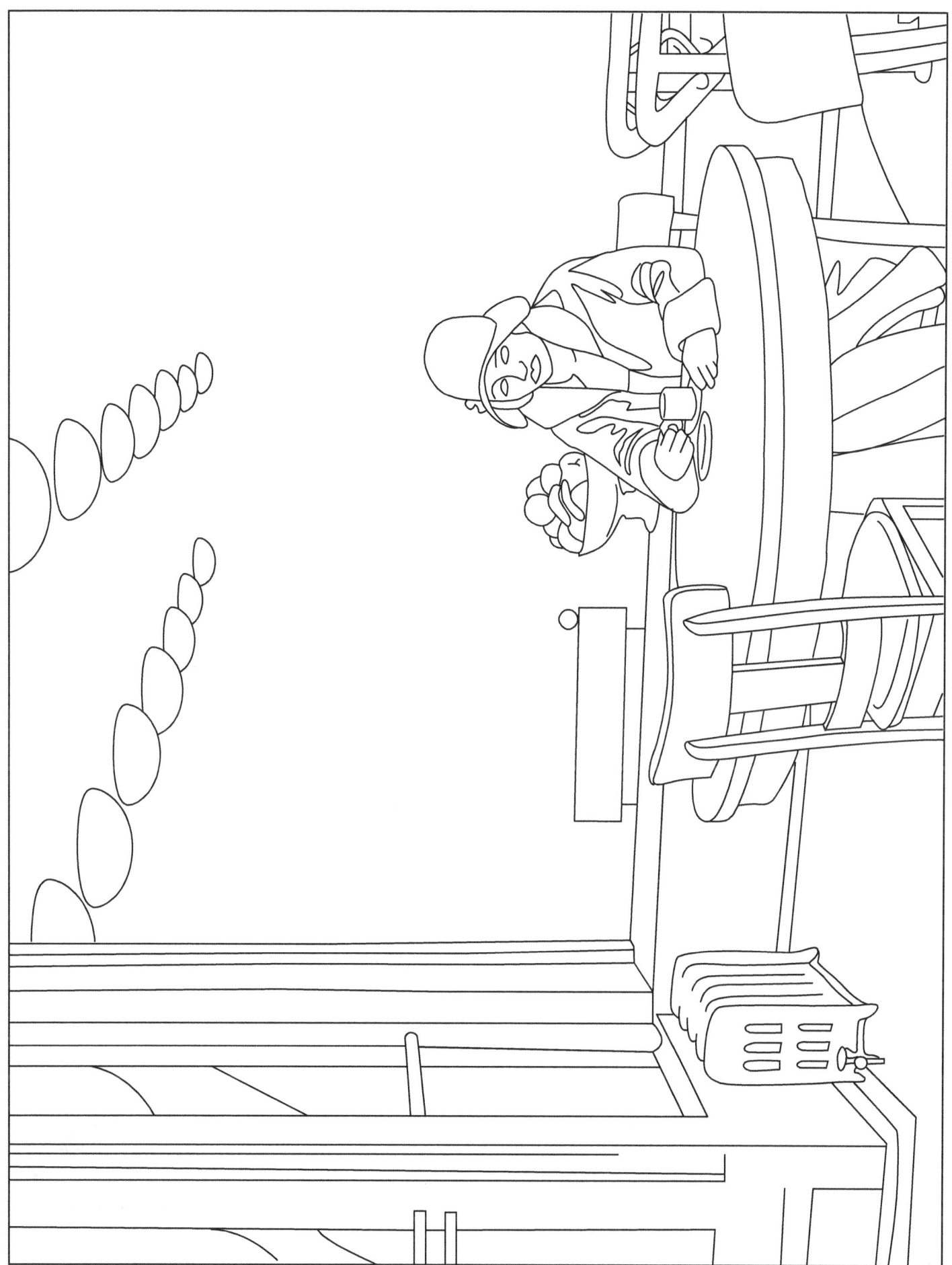

Yellow Blue
1963
Ellsworth Kelly (American, 1923 - 2015)

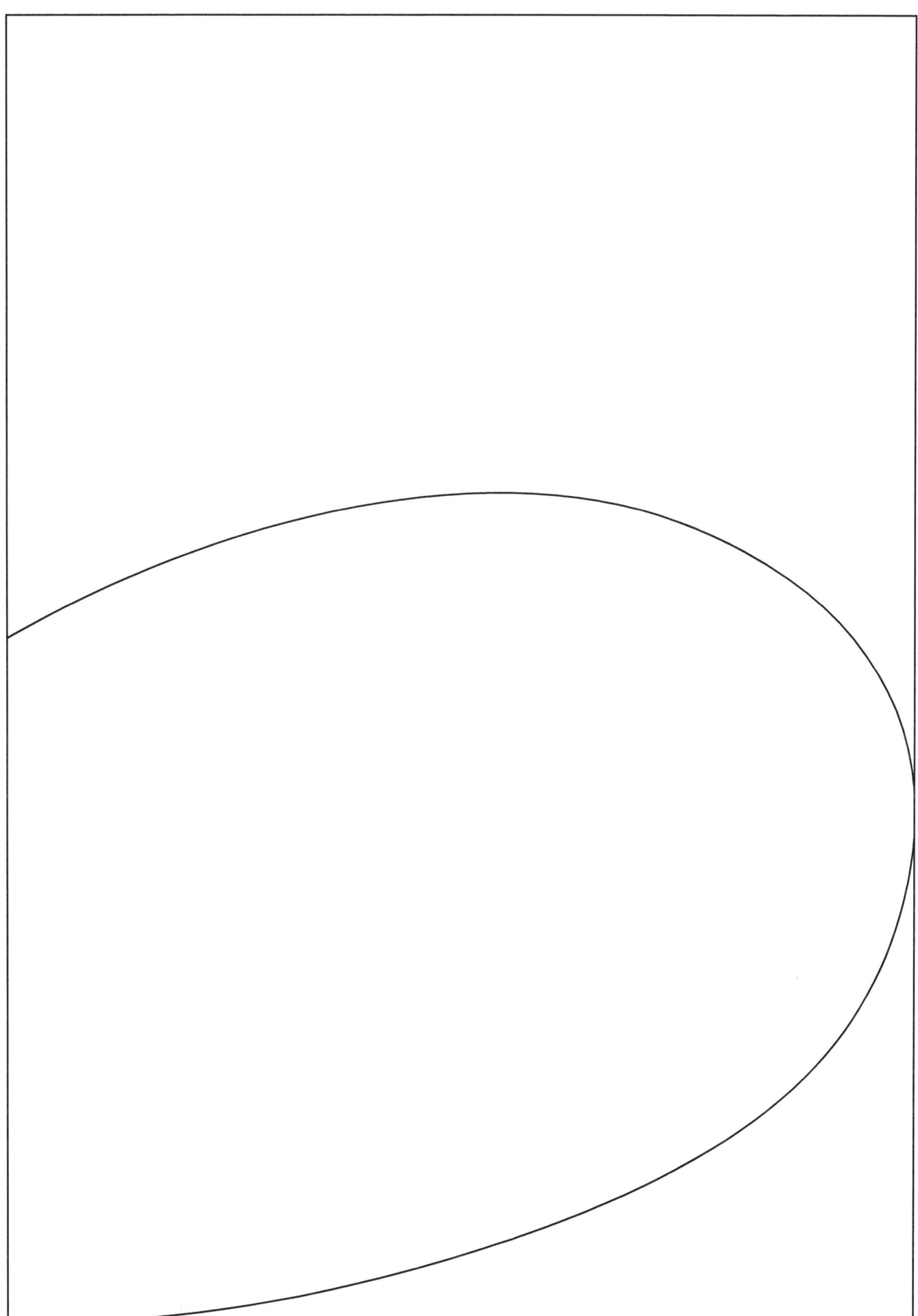

Memorial Day Run, Milwaukee
1966, printed 2006
Danny Lyon (American, born 1942)

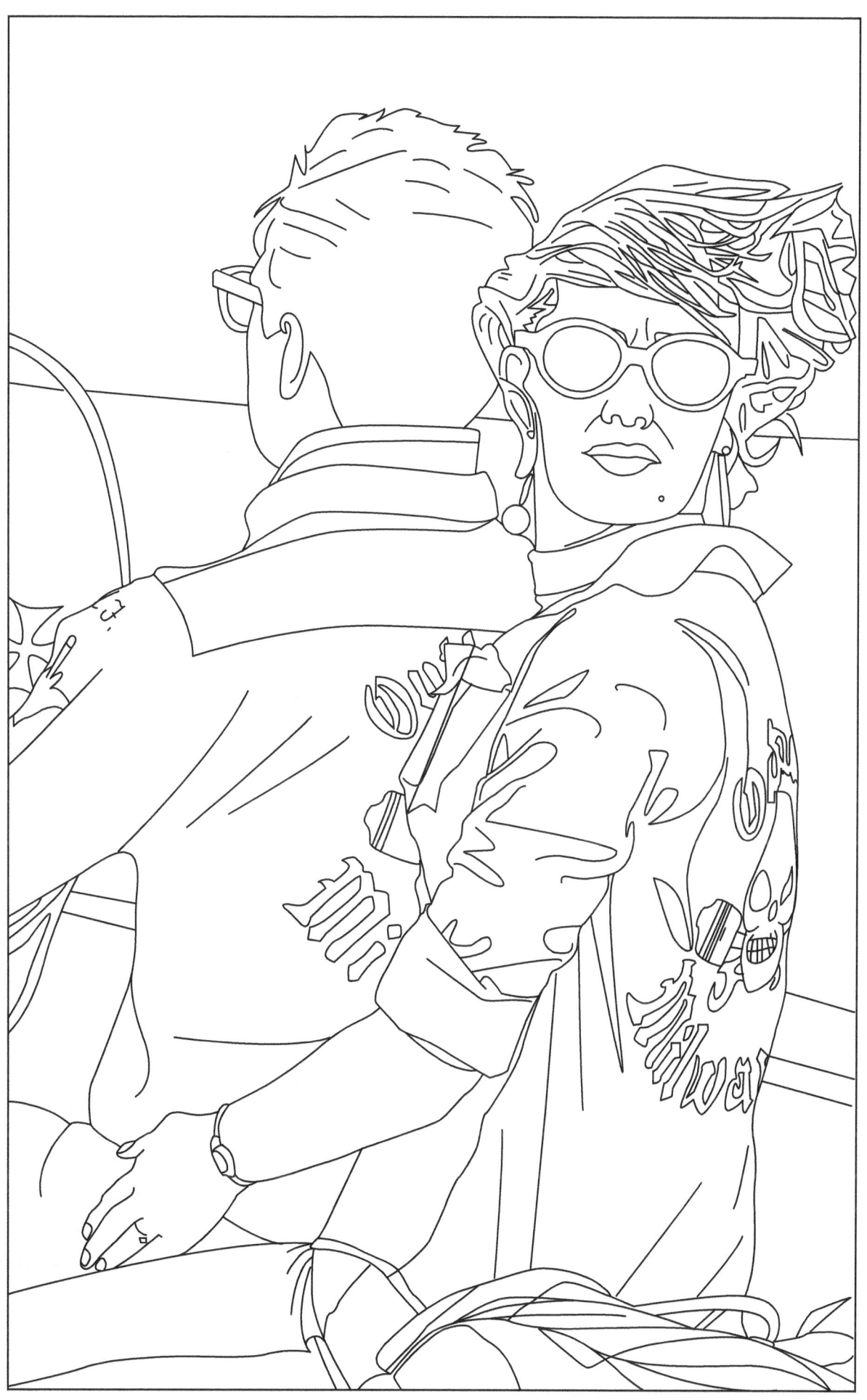

Untitled, plate 13, from "Etchasketchathon"
2005
Jake Chapman (British, born 1966)
Dinos Chapman (British, born 1962)

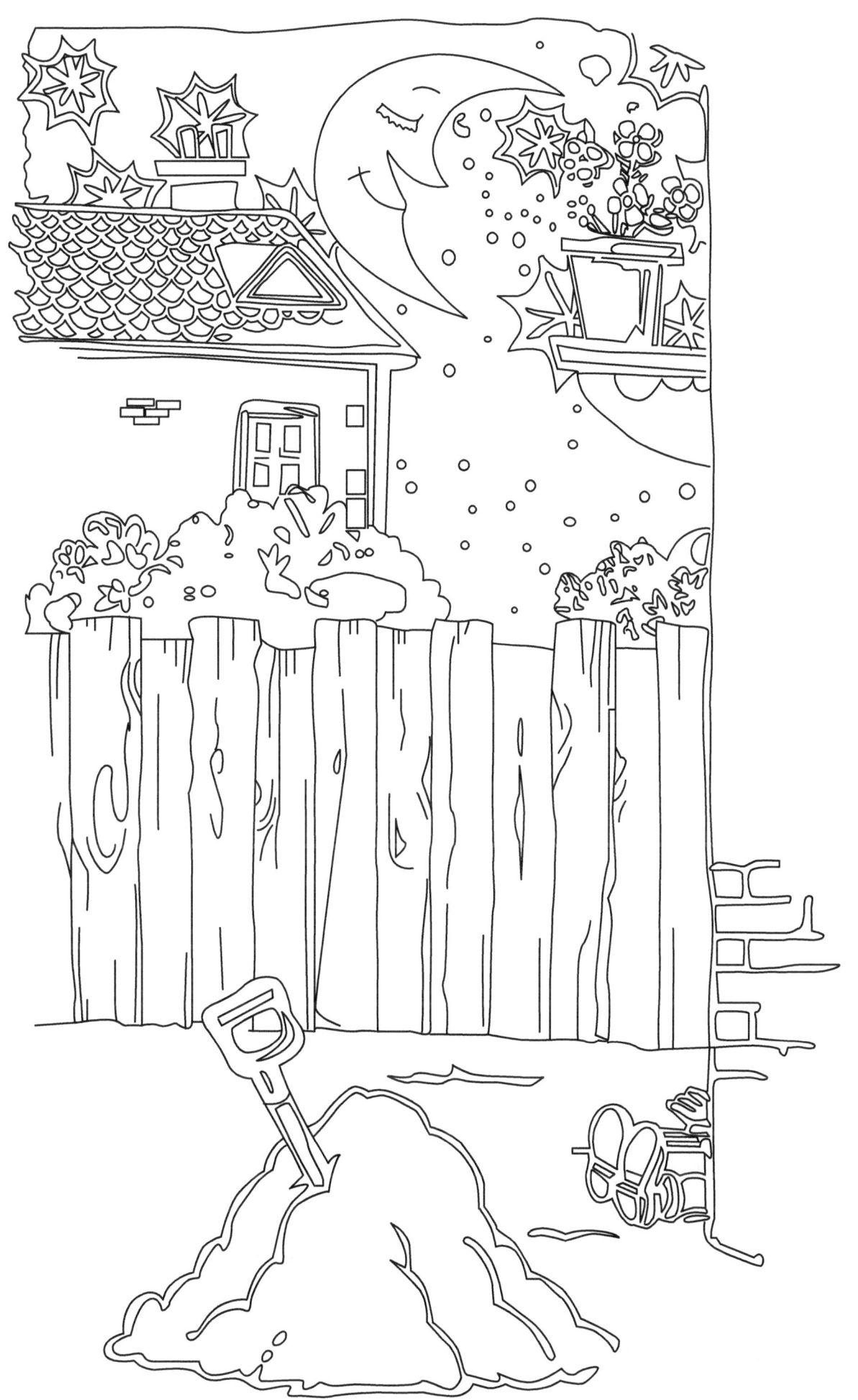

Le Villageois aux Cheveux Ras (The Villager with Close-Cropped Hair)
1947
Jean Dubuffet (French, 1901 - 1985)

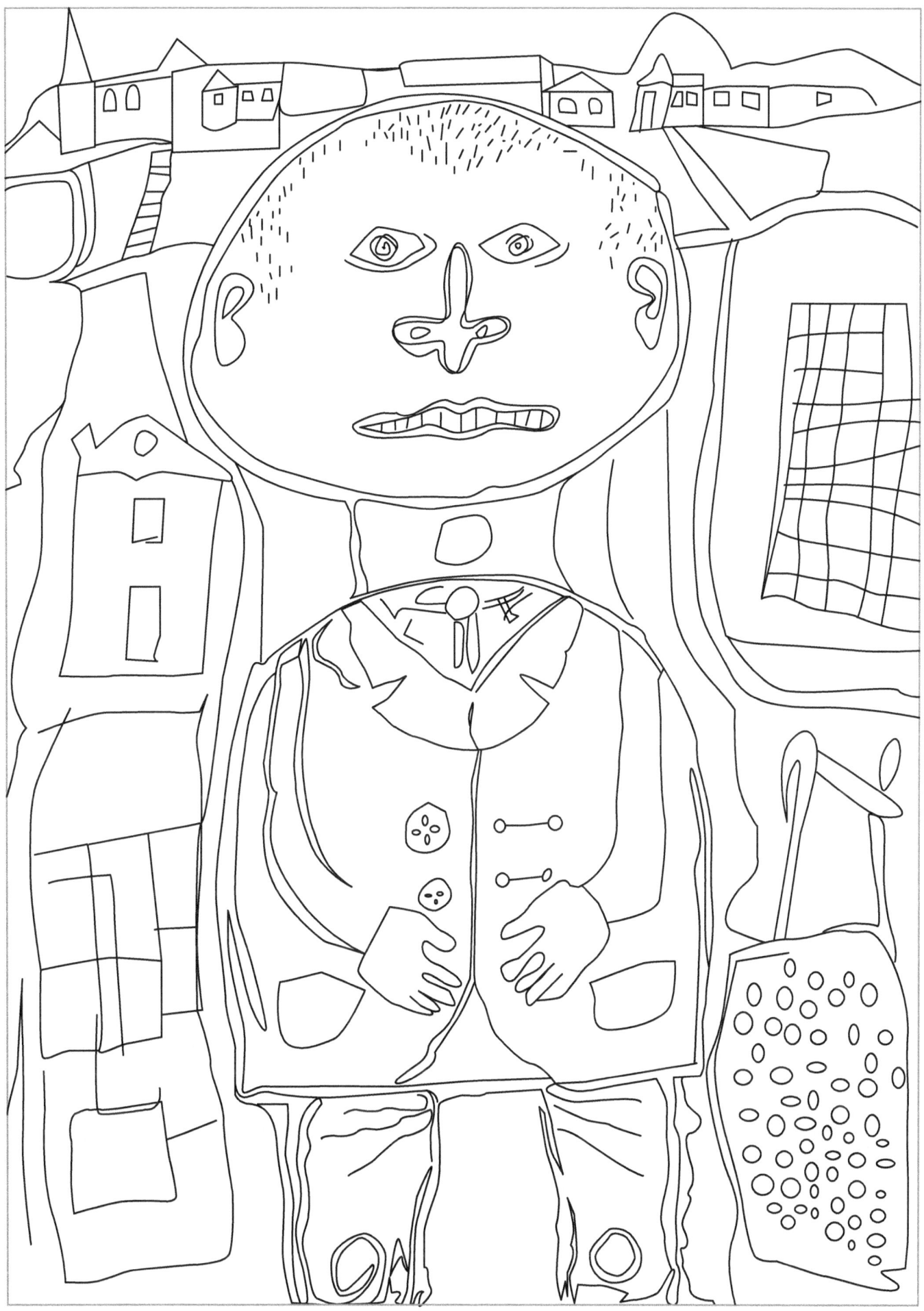

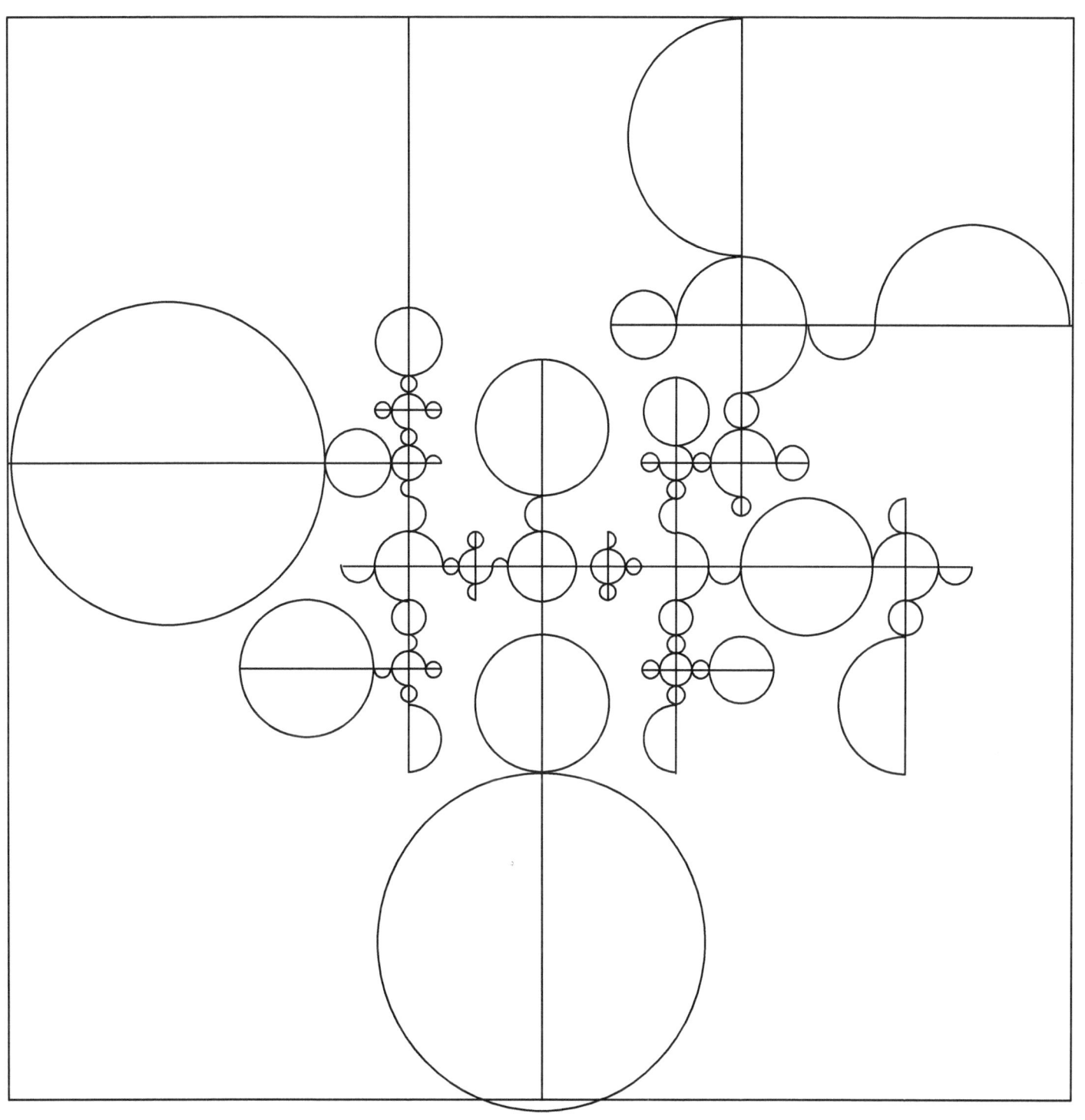

Samurai Tree (Invariant 1)
2005
Gabriel Orozco (Mexican, born 1962)

Untitled
2006
Tara Donovan (American, born 1969)

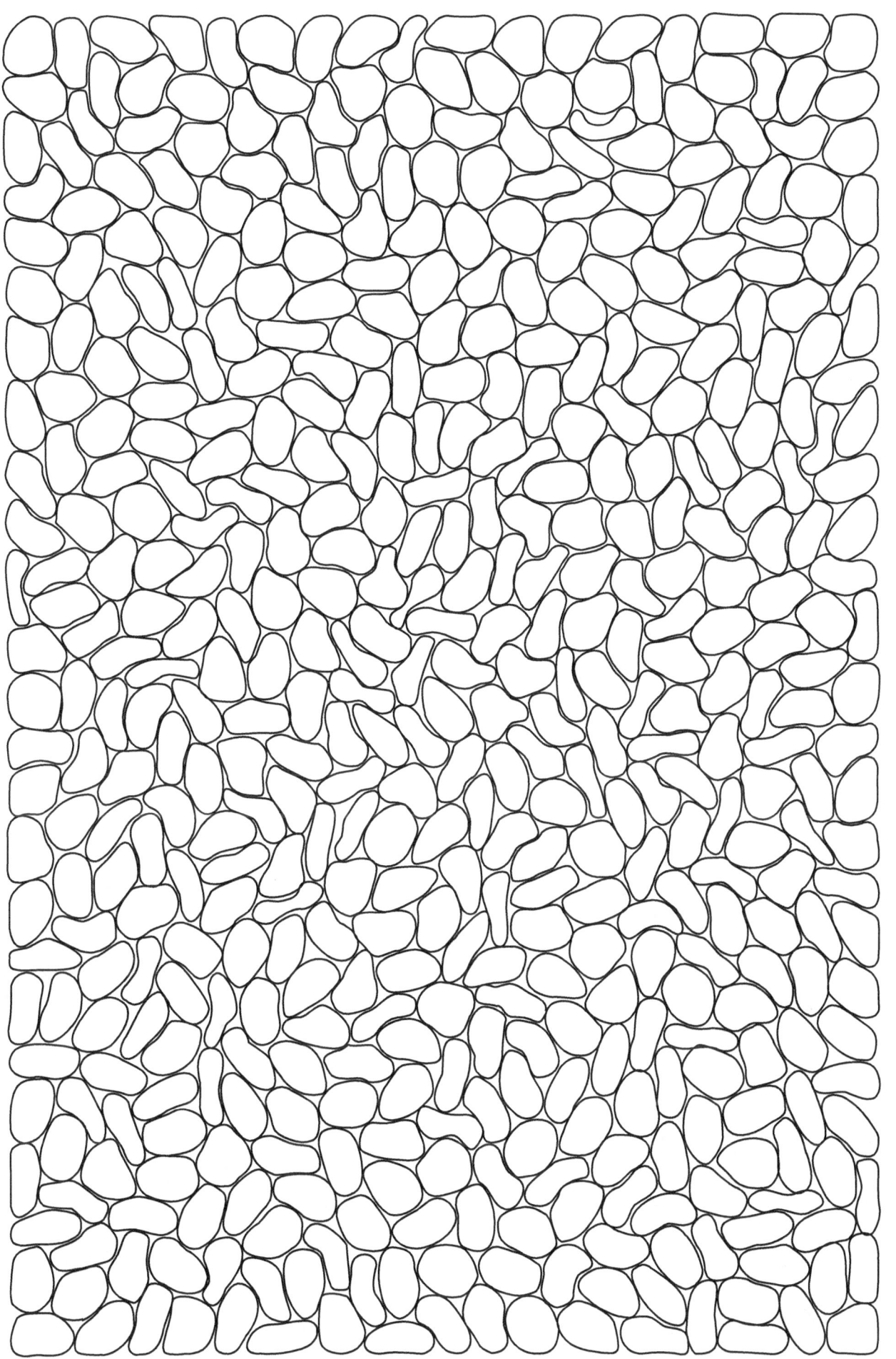

Dame à la robe blanche (Woman in White)
1946
Henri Matisse (French, 1869 - 1954)

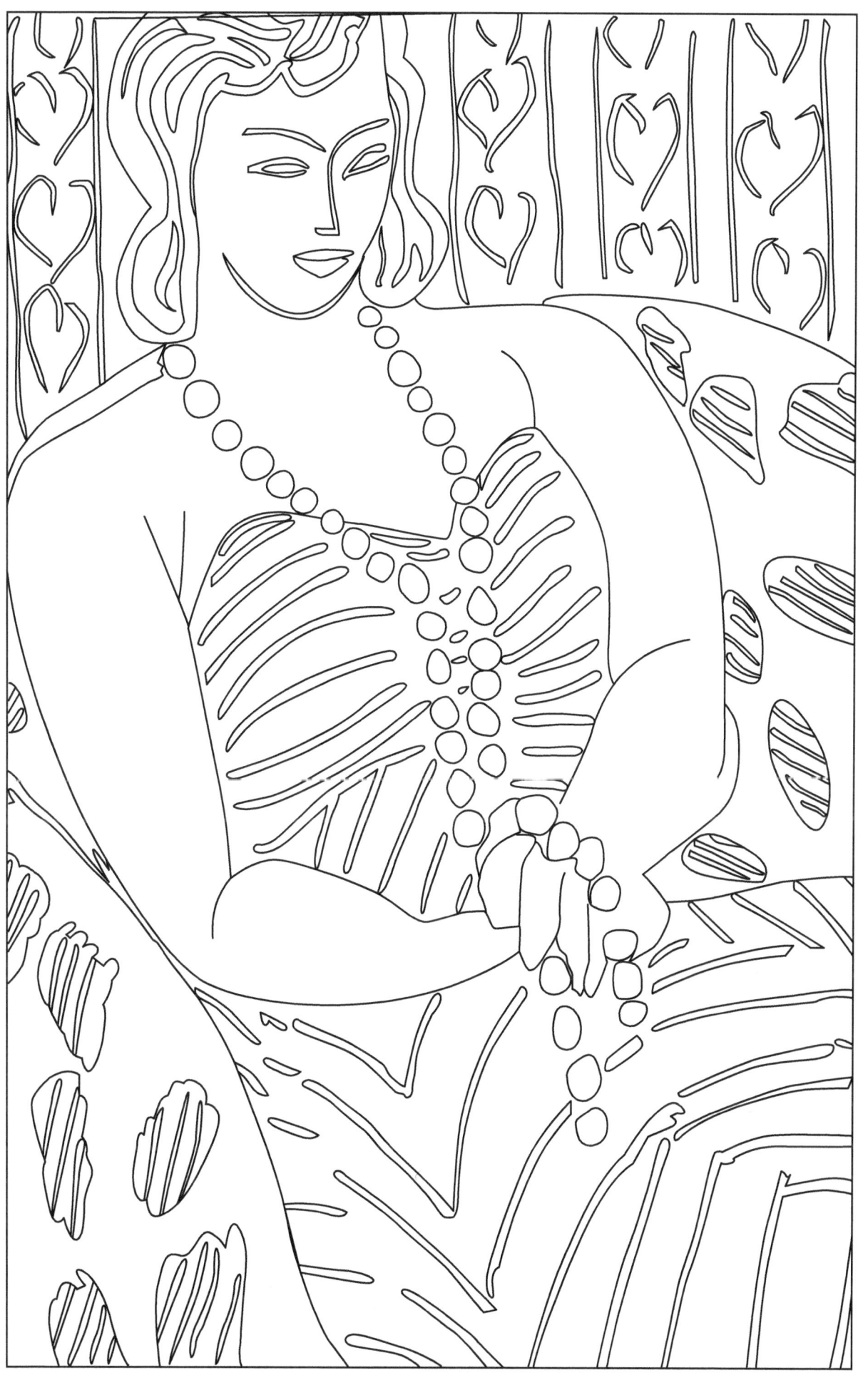

The Great Pyramid
1969

Roy Lichtenstein (American, 1923 - 1997)

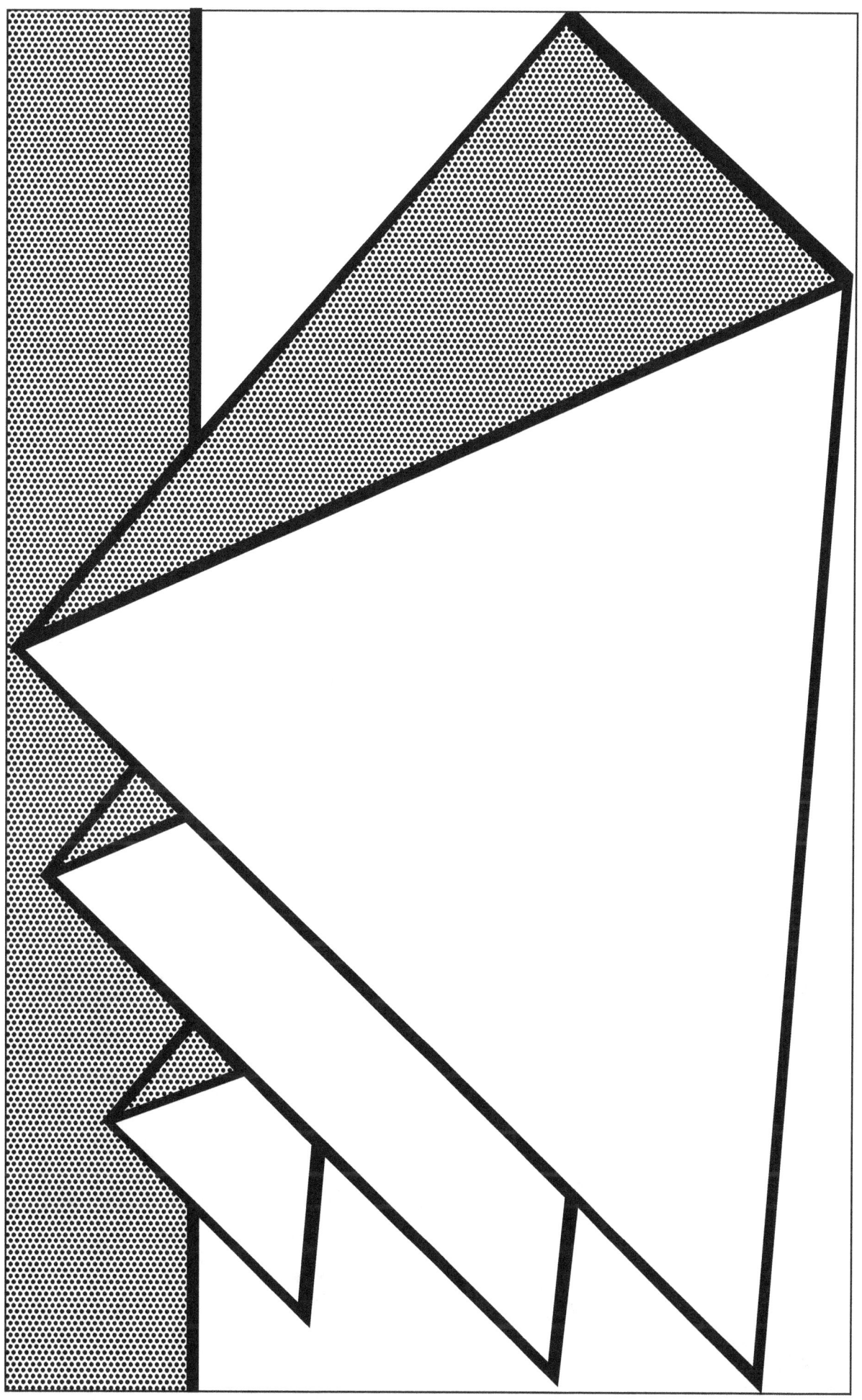